Mini Cakes

Mini Cakes

This edition published in 2011

LOVE FOOD is an imprint of Parragon Books Ltd

Parragon
Queen Street House
4 Queen Street
Bath BA1 1HE, UK

www.parragon.com

ISBN: 978-1-4454-4447-5

Printed in China

Created and produced by Pene Parker and Becca Spry
Author and home economist: Joanna Farrow
Photographer: Noel Murphy

Notes for the reader

This book uses both metric and imperial measurements. Follow the same units of measurements
throughout; do not mix metric and imperial. All spoon measurements are level: teaspoons are
assumed to be 5 ml, and tablespoons are assumed to be 15 ml. Unless otherwise stated, milk is
assumed to be full fat, eggs and individual vegetables are medium, and pepper is freshly ground
black pepper.

The times given are an approximate guide only. Preparation times differ according to the
techniques used by different people and the cooking times may also vary from those given.
Optional ingredients, variations or serving suggestions have not been included in the calculations.

Recipes using raw or very lightly cooked eggs should be avoided by infants, the elderly, pregnant
women, convalescents, and anyone suffering from an illness. Pregnant and breastfeeding women
are advised to avoid eating peanuts and peanut products. Sufferers from nut allergies should be
aware that some of the ready-made ingredients used in the recipes in this book may contain nuts.
Always check the packaging before use.

Contents

Introduction

Tiny portions of our favourite treats are so much fun to bake and eat. They're in great demand, perhaps because they have the 'cute factor' that large portions don't, or because they're so easy to pop into our mouths. From tiny little fruit loaves to miniature wedding cakes, this book of bite-sized morsels offers something for every occasion.

Equipment

A minimal amount of baking equipment is needed to make the cakes in this book. What you don't have already is widely available from cake-decorating stores or via the internet.

Mini cupcake and muffin cases
Mini cupcake and muffin paper cases tend to vary considerably in size. The recipes in this book require paper cases with a base diameter of 3 cm/1¼ inches and 4 cm/1½ inches. Mini silicone cases are also available in a variety of colours, from subtle to bright. They're dishwasher-proof and reusable, and cakes are easy to remove from them by peeling away the cases. To bake, simply set silicone cases on a baking tray rather than in a muffin tray or cupcake tray. Neither silicone cases nor paper cases need greasing.

Mini cupcake and muffin tins
Paper cupcake cases and muffin cases must sit comfortably in the tin's sections, which should offer some support but not crease the paper cases up. Mini cupcake tins and mini muffin tins both have 12 or 24 sections; if using a 12-section tin you will need to bake two batches of cakes for some recipes in this book.

Mini loaf tins
Mini loaves can be made in a 12-section silicone loaf tray with sections measuring 7 x 5 cm/3 x 2 inches. Alternatively they can be made in individual metal tins, but these are usually slightly larger, so you won't make as many cakes as the recipe states and you will need a little extra cooking time. Silicone trays don't need lining, but line each metal tin with a wide strip of baking paper that goes over the base and up the long sides.

Mini sectioned cake tins
Both round and square sectioned cake tins measure 5 cm/2 inches in diameter per section and are usually bought in packs of 16, which fit onto a base for baking. Alternatively bake a large sponge cake and let it firm up for 24 hours, then cut out 5-cm/2-inch rounds or squares using a metal cutter as a guide.

Metal cookie cutters
Cookie cutters can be used to cut out shapes from sponge cakes such as the moons on page 60. Cutters are available in a variety of shapes and sizes and are sometimes sold seasonally, so it's worth collecting your favourite shapes when you see them.

Small square cake tins
An 18-cm/7-inch square cake tin is a useful size for baking sponges to cut into small cakes. Grease and line the base and sides of the tin before baking.

Baking techniques

Preparing tins
Use greaseproof paper or baking paper to line tins and melted butter or vegetable oil to grease them.

Lining square tins
Place the tin on baking paper, draw around the tin and cut out the paper just inside the lines. Cut a strip the depth of the tin and make a 1-cm/½-inch fold along one long edge. Grease the tin using a pastry brush and fit the strip around the sides so the folded strip sits on the base. Snip the folded edge at the corners. Press the paper square into the base and grease the paper.

Lining round sectioned tins
Grease the sections. Cut out circles of baking paper 1 cm/½ inch larger than the section diameters. Make 5 mm/¼ inch cuts at the sides of the circles and press them in sections so the snipped edges go up the sides.

Mixing muffins
Muffins are made by adding the wet ingredients to the dry ingredients. The flour is usually sifted first. Add the wet ingredients all in one go and fold everything together gently. As soon as they're combined but with specks of flour still visible, spoon the mixture into the cases. Over-mixing muffins can make them less light.

Filling cases
Unless otherwise stated, fill cupcake cases until they're almost full and the mixture is level with the top of the cases. For muffins the mixture can extend above the tops of the cases slightly to achieve the 'muffin top'.

How to tell if a cake is cooked
Cakes are usually slightly domed in the centre with a lightly browned surface. Gently touch the surface with your flattened fingers; it should feel just firm. Some cakes require a further test of pushing a skewer into the centre; if cooked the skewer will come out clean.

Decorating techniques

Applying frostings and creams

Take a little of the frosting from the bowl using a small palette knife. Spread the frosting gently over each cake to cover it in an even layer before refining the application with the flat edge of the knife to level the surface.

Colouring ready-to-roll icing and marzipan

Using a cocktail stick, dot a little food colouring onto the icing paste. If you want a delicate colour, use a tiny amount as a little goes a long way. Working on a surface dusted with icing sugar, knead in the colour.

Covering cakes with ready-to-roll icing

Take the required amount of icing and roll it out thinly on a surface that is lightly dusted with icing sugar to between 3 mm/⅛ inch and 5 mm/¼ inch thick and 7 cm/2¾ inches in diameter. Lift over the cake and use your fingers to ease the icing around the sides, pinching it together where there's a point. Cut off the excess at these points and tuck the icing around the base before trimming off excess with a sharp knife.

Making a paper piping bag

Cut out a 25-cm/10-inch square from baking paper and fold it diagonally in half to make a triangle. Cut the paper in half, to one side of the folded line, to make two triangles. Holding one triangle with the long edge away from you, curl the right point over to meet the central point, forming a cone. Curl the left point over the cone. Adjust the points so there's no hole at the tip. Fold the points over to secure the cone in place.

Piping bags and nozzles

Piping bags can be fitted with nozzles or snipped at the tip. Half-fill the bag with icing and twist the open end together to seal. Snip off the tip and test the thickness of the piping, snipping off more if necessary. (If using a piping nozzle, cut 15 mm/½ inch off the tip of the bag and fit with a nozzle before filling and sealing.) The nozzles used in this book are: a large star nozzle for lavish swirls; a small star nozzle for small stars or shells; and a writer nozzle for lines and dots.

Vanilla sponge cake

Makes: 1 x 18-cm/7-inch
round or square cake
Prep: 15 minutes
Cook: 40 minutes

150 g/5½ oz lightly salted
butter, softened

150 g/5½ oz caster sugar

1 tsp vanilla extract

3 eggs, beaten

175 g/6 oz self-raising flour

2 tbsp milk

When using this moist, buttery sponge cake mixture, follow the baking directions in your chosen recipe. To bake it as a sponge cake, put it in an 18-cm/ 7-inch round or square greased and lined cake tin and bake for 40 minutes, or until firm to touch.

1. Put the butter and sugar in a mixing bowl and beat them together with an electric handheld whisk until pale and fluffy. Beat in the vanilla. Add the eggs, a little at a time, beating between each addition. (If they are added too quickly, the mixture will separate and the cake won't be as light.)

2. Sift in the flour, then stir it in gently with a metal spoon. As soon as the ingredients are combined, gently stir in the milk. The mixture should drop easily from the spoon when tapped on the side of the bowl. (For a shortcut 'all in one' method, put all the ingredients in the bowl together and beat until soft and creamy.) Cook as per your recipe or turn the mixture out into a greased and lined 18-cm/7-inch cake tin and bake in an oven preheated to 180°C/350°F/Gas Mark 4 for 40 minutes.

Variations

White chocolate: Replace half the sugar with 200 g/7 oz melted white chocolate, stirring it into the mixture after the eggs.

Lemon: Add the finely grated rind of 2 lemons when creaming the butter and sugar and use 2 tablespoons of lemon juice instead of vanilla and milk.

Orange: Add the finely grated rind of 1 orange when creaming the butter and sugar and use 2 tablespoons of orange juice instead of vanilla and milk.

Almond: Replace 55 g/2 oz flour with 55 g/2 oz ground almonds and add 1 teaspoon of almond extract instead of the vanilla.

Buttercream

Makes: 1 quantity of
buttercream

Put 100 g/3½ oz unsalted butter in a mixing bowl and beat with an electric handheld whisk until softened. Add 150 g/5½ oz icing sugar and beat, using the whisk, until smooth and creamy. Pour in 1 tablespoon of hot water and beat again until very soft and fluffy. For vanilla buttercream beat in 1 teaspoon of vanilla extract with the icing sugar. For lemon buttercream beat in the finely grated rind of 1 lemon with the icing sugar and use 2 tablespoons of lemon juice instead of the water.

Mini Classic Cakes

Carrot cakes

Makes: 20
Prep: 1 hour, plus cooling
Cook: 35 minutes

Carrot cake is such an all-time favourite, it quite simply had to be included here. If you're making these in advance, the little marzipan carrots can be positioned after frosting the cake, but don't add the leafy tops more than a few hours before serving as they are likely to wilt.

150 g/5½ oz lightly salted butter, softened, plus extra for greasing

150 g/5½ oz light muscovado sugar

3 eggs

150 g/5½ oz self-raising flour

½ tsp baking powder

½ tsp ground mixed spice

85 g/3 oz ground almonds

finely grated rind of 1 lemon

150 g/5½ oz carrots, grated

85 g/3 oz sultanas, roughly chopped

DECORATION

150 g/5½ oz cream cheese

40 g/1½ oz unsalted butter, softened

115 g/4 oz icing sugar, plus extra for dusting

2 tbsp lemon juice

60 g/2¼ oz marzipan

orange food colouring

several sprigs of dill

1. Preheat the oven to 180°C/350°F/Gas Mark 4. Grease and line the base and sides of a 26-cm x 22-cm/10-inch x 8-inch roasting tin or similar sized tin. Grease the baking paper. Put the butter, light muscovado sugar, eggs, flour, baking powder, mixed spice, almonds and lemon rind in a mixing bowl and beat together with an electric handheld whisk until smooth and creamy. Stir in the carrots and sultanas.

2. Turn the mixture out into the tin and level the surface. Bake in the preheated oven for 35 minutes, or until risen and just firm to the touch. Leave in the tin for 10 minutes, then transfer to a wire rack to cool.

3. For the decoration, beat together the cream cheese, butter, icing sugar and lemon juice until creamy. Colour the marzipan deep orange (see page 8). Roll it into a sausage shape on a surface lightly dusted with icing sugar, then divide it into 20 pieces and form each one into a small carrot shape, marking shallow grooves around each with a knife.

4. Using a palette knife, spread the frosting over the cake, taking it almost to the edges. Trim the crusts from the cake to neaten it, then cut it into 20 squares. Place a marzipan carrot on each cake and add a small sprig of dill.

Cherry and almond loaves

Makes: 12
Prep: 15 minutes, plus cooling
Cook: 20 minutes

A bite-sized mini treat for those who like traditional cakes. If you don't have a silicone loaf tray, use individual metal tins (see page 6) – they're slightly larger and you'll have enough mixture for about 8 cakes, which will need an extra 5 minutes' cooking time.

85 g/3 oz lightly salted butter, softened, plus extra for greasing

70 g/2½ oz caster sugar

1 egg

1 egg yolk

70 g/2½ oz self-raising flour

½ tsp almond extract

55 g/2 oz ground almonds

55 g/2 oz natural glacé cherries, roughly chopped

2 tbsp flaked almonds

55 g/2 oz icing sugar

2 tsp lemon juice

1. Preheat the oven to 180°C/350°F/Gas Mark 4. Place a 12-section silicone mini loaf tray on a baking tray, or grease and base-line individual mini loaf tins. Put the butter, caster sugar, egg, egg yolk, flour, almond extract and ground almonds in a mixing bowl and beat together with an electric hand-held whisk until smooth and creamy. Stir in the cherries.

2. Using a teaspoon, spoon the mixture into the tray sections and level with the back of the spoon. Break up the flaked almonds slightly by squeezing them in your hands and scatter them over the cake mixture. Bake in the preheated oven for 20 minutes (25 minutes if using tins), or until risen and just firm to the touch. Leave in the tray for 5 minutes, then transfer to a wire rack to cool.

3. Beat the icing sugar and lemon juice together in a small bowl and drizzle over the cakes with a teaspoon. Leave to set.

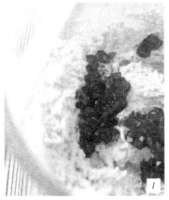

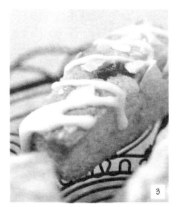

Mango cakes

Makes: 12
Prep: 15 minutes, plus cooling,
plus 2–3 hours soaking
Cook: 20 minutes

70 g/2½ oz dried mango, finely
chopped

finely grated rind of 1 orange,
plus 3 tbsp juice

25 g/1 oz creamed coconut

85 g/3 oz lightly salted butter,
softened, plus extra for greasing

70 g/2½ oz caster sugar

1 egg

85 g/3 oz self-raising flour

icing sugar, for dusting

Dried mango and creamed coconut give these little tea cakes a fresh, tropical flavour, heightened by a subtle hint of orange. Moist and buttery, they'll keep in an airtight container for several days.

1. Preheat the oven to 180°C/350°F/Gas Mark 4. Place a 12-section silicone mini loaf tray on a baking tray, or grease and base-line individual mini loaf tins. Put the mango and orange juice in a small bowl and leave to stand, covered, for 2–3 hours, or until the orange juice is mostly absorbed. Finely grate the coconut (if it's very firm and difficult to grate, warm it briefly in the microwave first).

2. Put the coconut, butter, sugar, egg, flour and orange rind in a mixing bowl and beat together with an electric handheld whisk until smooth and pale. Stir in the mango and any unabsorbed orange juice.

3. Using a teaspoon, spoon the mixture into the tray sections and level with the back of the spoon. Bake in the preheated oven for 20 minutes (25 minutes if using tins), or until risen and just firm to the touch. Leave in the tray for 5 minutes, then transfer to a wire rack to cool.

4. Serve lightly dusted with icing sugar.

Mini Victoria sandwich cakes

Makes: 12
Prep: 20 minutes, plus cooling
Cook: 15 minutes

So tiny and dainty, these 'doll's house'-sized sponges are just right with a cup of tea when you don't want anything too rich or filling. Because of their size they'll dry out quickly, so store them in an airtight container or freeze if making ahead.

70 g/2½ oz lightly salted butter, softened, plus extra for greasing

70 g/2½ oz caster sugar

70 g/2½ oz self-raising flour

1 egg

1 egg yolk

1 tsp vanilla extract

DECORATION

150 ml/5 fl oz double cream

6 tbsp strawberry jam

85 g/3 oz icing sugar

1 tbsp lemon juice

1. Preheat the oven to 180°C/350°F/Gas Mark 4. Place a 12-section silicone mini muffin tray on a baking tray, or grease and base-line a 12-section mini muffin tin. Put the butter, caster sugar, flour, egg, egg yolk and vanilla in a mixing bowl and beat together with an electric handheld whisk until it is smooth and creamy.

2. Using a teaspoon, spoon the mixture into the tray sections and level with the back of the spoon. Bake in the preheated oven for 15 minutes, or until risen and just firm to the touch. Leave in the tray for 5 minutes, then transfer to a wire rack to cool.

3. For the decoration, whip the cream until it just peaks. Split the cakes in half horizontally using a small serrated knife. Press 2 tablespoons of the jam through a small sieve into a bowl to extract the seeds. Put the sieved jam in a small paper piping bag and snip off the tip (see page 8). Sandwich the cakes together with the remaining jam and cream.

4. Beat the icing sugar and lemon juice together in a bowl until smooth. Spoon the icing over the cakes, spreading it just to the edges. Pipe dots of jam on top of each cake and draw a wooden skewer through them.

Iced baby bundt cakes

Makes: 12
Prep: 20 minutes, plus cooling
Cook: 15-20 minutes

This bundt recipe is made with cinnamon, walnuts and apples for a really moist texture. Don't be put off if you don't have mini bundt tins; any small tins with a similar capacity can be used just as effectively.

200 g/7 oz plain flour, plus extra for sprinkling

1 tsp baking powder

1 tsp ground cinnamon, plus extra for sprinkling

125 g/4½ oz caster sugar

60 g/2¼ oz walnuts, finely chopped

2 small dessert apples, peeled, cored and finely grated

6 tbsp vegetable oil, plus extra for greasing

3 eggs

150 ml/5 fl oz buttermilk

ICING

3 tbsp natural yogurt

150 g/5½ oz icing sugar, sifted

1. Preheat the oven to 180°C/350°F/Gas Mark 4. Brush 2 x 75-ml/2½-fl oz mini bundt tins with vegetable oil. Sprinkle a little flour into the tins and tilt so that both the bases and sides are coated; tap out the excess.

2. Sift the flour, baking powder and cinnamon into a mixing bowl. Stir in the caster sugar, walnuts and apples.

3. In a separate mixing bowl, beat together the oil, eggs and buttermilk. Add them to the dry ingredients and mix to form a soft paste.

4. Using a teaspoon, spoon the mixture into the tins and level with the back of the spoon. Bake in the preheated oven for 15–20 minutes, or until risen and just firm to the touch. Leave in the tins for 5 minutes, then transfer to a wire rack to cool.

5. For the icing, put the yogurt into a bowl and add the icing sugar. Beat together well until smooth. Spoon a little of the icing onto the top of each cake, easing it slightly down the sides with the back of the spoon so the icing runs down the flutes around the sides. Lightly sprinkle the tops of the cakes with cinnamon.

Coffee crumb cakes

Makes: 18
Prep: 30 minutes, plus cooling
Cook: 30–35 minutes

55 g/2 oz lightly salted butter,
softened, plus extra for greasing

100 g/3½ oz caster sugar

1 egg

5 tbsp soured cream

125 g/4½ oz self-raising flour

TOPPING

85 g/3 oz plain flour

70 g/2½ oz lightly salted butter,
cut into pieces

½ tsp ground mixed spice

1½ tsp ground espresso coffee

70 g/2½ oz caster sugar

ICING

85 g/3 oz icing sugar

1 tbsp strong espresso coffee

One of these treats is an ideal accompaniment to a mid-morning cup of tea or coffee. The crumb topping is sweet and streusel-like, in delicious contrast to the light and airy sponge underneath it.

1. Preheat the oven to 180°C/350°F/Gas Mark 4. Grease and line the base and sides of an 18-cm/7-inch shallow, loose-bottomed square cake tin. Grease the baking paper.

2. For the topping, put the plain flour, butter, mixed spice and coffee in a food processor and blend until the mixture starts to resemble coarse breadcrumbs. Add the caster sugar and blend again briefly. Tip the mixture into a mixing bowl.

3. For the sponge, put the butter, caster sugar, egg, soured cream and self-raising flour in the food processor and blend until smooth and creamy, then turn out into the tin and level the surface. Sprinkle the crumb mixture in an even layer on top. Bake in the preheated oven for 30–35 minutes, or until risen and just firm to the touch and a skewer inserted into the centre comes out clean. Leave in the tin for 10 minutes, then transfer to a wire rack to cool.

4. For the icing, put all but 2 tablespoons of the icing sugar in a small mixing bowl and add the coffee. Beat to a smooth paste that falls in a thick trail from the spoon, adding a little more icing sugar if necessary. Cut the cake into 3 even-sized pieces, then cut across to make 18 rectangular pieces. Drizzle with the icing.

Gooey chocolate fudge bites

Makes: 21
Prep: 25 minutes, plus cooling
Cook: 35 minutes

200 g/7 oz lightly salted butter,
cut into pieces, plus extra for
greasing

200 g/7 oz plain chocolate,
roughly chopped

100 ml/3½ fl oz double cream

3 eggs

150 g/5½ oz light muscovado
sugar

100 g/3½ oz self-raising flour

ICING

200 g/7 oz plain chocolate

3 tbsp golden syrup

55 g/2 oz unsalted butter, cut
into pieces

70 g/2½ oz icing sugar, sifted

This is as rich and delicious as chocolate cake can be! It's moist and gooey, with a generous amount of chocolate fudge icing. Store in a cool place rather than in the fridge so that the texture doesn't spoil.

1. Preheat the oven to 160°C/325°F/Gas Mark 3. Grease and line the base and sides of a 20-cm/8-inch square cake tin. Grease the baking paper.

2. Put the butter, chocolate and cream in a heatproof bowl, set the bowl over a saucepan of gently simmering water and heat until melted. Leave to cool slightly.

3. Put the eggs and light muscovado sugar in a mixing bowl and beat together with an electric handheld whisk until the mixture begins to turn frothy. Stir in the cooled chocolate mixture. Sift in the flour and stir it in gently.

4. Turn the mixure into the tin and level the surface. Bake in the preheated oven for 35 minutes, or until risen and just firm to the touch. Leave in the tin for 10 minutes, then transfer to a wire rack to cool.

5. For the icing, put 175 g/6 oz of the chocolate in a small heavy-bottomed saucepan with the syrup and butter. Heat gently, stirring frequently, until the mixture is smooth and glossy. Transfer the mixture to a mixing bowl and beat in the icing sugar. Leave until the icing has thickened enough to just hold its shape.

6. Split the cake in half horizontally and spread half the fudge icing on the cut side of the bottom piece. Place the other piece on top, cut-side down, and spread the remaining icing on top of the cake. Using a sharp knife, carefully cut thin shards from the remaining chocolate. (If it's too brittle, heat very briefly in the microwave and try again.) Trim off the edges of the cake to neaten it, then cut it into 21 rectangles. Scatter the shards on top.

Chocolate brownies

Makes: 25
Prep: 15 minutes, plus cooling
Cook: 18–20 minutes

These little brownies have the familiar sugary crust and soft gooey centre that we've come to know and love. They're impossible to resist, so it's a good thing they're only bite-sized!

115 g/4 oz lightly salted butter, cut into pieces, plus extra for greasing

100 g/3½ oz plain chocolate, roughly chopped

2 eggs

175 g/6 oz light muscovado sugar

2 tsp vanilla extract

55 g/2 oz plain flour

25 g/1 oz cocoa powder

40 g/1½ oz pecan or walnuts, roughly chopped

1. Preheat the oven to 200°C/400°F/Gas Mark 6. Grease and line the base and sides of an 18-cm/7-inch shallow, loose-bottomed square cake tin.

2. Put the butter and chocolate in a heatproof bowl, set the bowl over a saucepan of gently simmering water and heat until melted. Leave the mixture to cool slightly.

3. Put the eggs, sugar and vanilla in a mixing bowl and beat together with an electric handheld whisk until the mixture begins to turn frothy. Stir in the chocolate mixture until combined.

4 Sift the flour and cocoa powder into the bowl and scatter in the nuts. Stir together gently, then turn the mixture into the tin and level the surface.

5. Bake in the preheated oven for 18–20 minutes, or until the crust feels dry but gives a little when gently pressed. (If you're unsure, it's better to slightly under-cook brownies as they lose their gooeyness when they are over-baked.) Leave in the tin for 10 minutes, then transfer to a wire rack to cool. Cut the cake into 25 squares.

3

4

5

Vanilla swirled brownies

Makes: 12
Prep: 20 minutes, plus cooling
Cook: 12–15 minutes

85 g/3 oz lightly salted butter,
plus extra for greasing

100 g/3½ oz plain chocolate,
roughly chopped

1 egg

1 egg yolk

100 g/3½ oz light muscovado
sugar

40 g/1½ oz self-raising flour

¼ tsp baking powder

85 g/3 oz milk chocolate, roughly
chopped

FROSTING

150 g/5½ oz mascarpone cheese

4 tbsp icing sugar

1 tsp vanilla extract

milk or plain chocolate curls,
to sprinkle

These rich, chocolatey morsels are great as a teatime treat — and even better with coffee after a special dinner with friends.

1. Preheat the oven to 190°C/375°F/Gas Mark 5. Grease and base-line a 12-section mini muffin tin.

2. Put the butter and plain chocolate in a heatproof bowl, set the bowl over a saucepan of gently simmering water and heat until melted. Leave the mixture to cool slightly.

3. Put the egg, egg yolk and light muscovado sugar in a mixing bowl and beat together with an electric handheld whisk until the mixture begins to turn frothy. Stir in the melted chocolate. Sift the flour and baking powder into the bowl, scatter in the milk chocolate and stir together. Using a teaspoon, spoon the mixture into the tray sections.

4. Bake in the preheated oven for 12–15 minutes, or until the crust feels dry but gives a little when gently pressed. (If you're unsure, it's better to slightly under-cook brownies as they lose their gooeyness when over-baked.) Leave in the tray for 10 minutes, then transfer to a wire rack to cool.

5. For the frosting, put the mascarpone cheese, icing sugar and vanilla in a small bowl and beat with an electric handheld whisk until smooth and creamy. Put the mixture in a piping bag fitted with a 1-cm/½-inch star nozzle and pipe swirls over the cakes. Sprinkle with chocolate curls.

Tiny Muffins and Cupcakes

Blueberry and vanilla muffins

Makes: 18
Prep: 10 minutes, plus cooling
Cook: 15 minutes

In these fresh blueberry muffins, the plump, juicy fruits burst during baking to colour and flavour the light, airy sponge. This recipe uses homemade paper cases, made by pressing squares of baking paper into the muffin tray.

125 g/4½ oz self-raising flour

½ tsp baking powder

70 g/2½ oz caster sugar

85 g/3 oz blueberries

2 tsp vanilla extract

1 egg

125 ml/4 fl oz buttermilk

2 tbsp vegetable oil

vanilla sugar, for dusting

1. Preheat the oven to 190°C/375°F/Gas Mark 5. Cut out 18 x 9-cm/3½-inch squares from baking paper. Push the squares into 2 x 12-section mini muffin tins, creasing the squares to fit so that they form paper cases. Don't worry if they lift out of the sections slightly; the weight of the muffin mixture will hold them in place.

2. Sift the flour and baking powder into a mixing bowl. Stir in the sugar and blueberries. In a separate mixing bowl, beat together the vanilla, egg, buttermilk and oil with a fork until evenly combined.

3. Tip the buttermilk mixture into the flour. Using a dessertspoon, gently fold the ingredients together until only just mixed. (Don't over-blend the ingredients or the muffins won't be as light.)

4. Spoon the mixture into the paper cases; it should be level with the top of the tin. Sprinkle with a little vanilla sugar and bake in the preheated oven for 15 minutes, or until risen and just firm to the touch. Leave the muffins in the tin for 2 minutes, then transfer them in their cases to a wire rack to cool. Serve warm or cold, dusted with extra vanilla sugar.

1

3

4

Cranberry muffins

Makes: 18
Prep: 10 minutes, plus cooling
Cook: 12–15 minutes

These muffins can be prepared and baked in less than half an hour, perfect for a relaxed weekend breakfast. For flavour variations, try adding the grated rind of an orange or a sprinkling of ground ginger or cinnamon.

100 g/3½ oz self-raising flour

½ tsp baking powder

55 g/2 oz caster sugar

100 g/3½ oz dried cranberries, roughly chopped

100 ml/3½ fl oz natural yogurt

1 egg

2 tbsp vegetable oil

icing sugar, for dusting

1. Preheat the oven to 190°C/375°F/Gas Mark 5. Line 2 x 12-section mini muffin tins with 18 x 3-cm/1¼-inch mini paper cases.

2. Sift the flour and baking powder into a mixing bowl. Stir in the caster sugar and cranberries. In a separate mixing bowl, beat together the yogurt, egg and vegetable oil with a fork until evenly combined.

3. Tip the yogurt mixture into the flour. Using a dessertspoon, gently fold the ingredients together until only just mixed. (Don't over-blend the ingredients or the muffins won't be as light.)

4. Spoon the mixture into the paper cases; it should be level with the top of the tin. Bake in the preheated oven for 12–15 minutes, or until risen and just firm to the touch. Leave the muffins in the tin for 2 minutes, then transfer them in their cases to a wire rack to cool. Serve warm or cold, dusted with icing sugar.

Double chocolate muffins

Makes: 12
Prep: 15 minutes, plus cooling
Cook: 15 minutes

Because these muffins are tiny, it's only right that they're as packed with chocolate as they could be! Any that are not eaten fresh from the oven can be kept for two days in an airtight container. Warm them for a few minutes in a moderate oven to revive their flavour.

15 g/½ oz cocoa powder

70 g/2½ oz self-raising flour

¼ tsp baking powder

25 g/1 oz light muscovado sugar

85 g/3 oz milk chocolate,
roughly chopped

1 egg

3 tbsp milk

40 g/1½ oz lightly salted butter,
melted

40 g/1½ oz plain chocolate,
roughly chopped

1. Preheat the oven to 190°C/375°F/Gas Mark 5. Line a 12-section mini muffin tin with 3-cm/1¼-inch mini paper cases.

2. Sift the cocoa powder, flour and baking powder into a mixing bowl. Stir in the light muscovado sugar and milk chocolate. In a separate mixing bowl, beat together the egg, milk and butter with a fork until they are evenly combined.

3. Tip the egg mixture into the flour. Using a dessertspoon, gently fold the ingredients together until only just mixed. (Don't over-blend the ingredients or the muffins won't be as light.)

4. Spoon the mixture into the paper cases; it should be level with the top of the tin. Bake in the preheated oven for 15 minutes, or until risen and just firm to the touch. Leave the muffins in the tin for 2 minutes, then transfer them in their cases to a wire rack to cool.

5. Put the plain chocolate in a heatproof bowl, set over a saucepan of gently simmering water and heat until melted. Using a teaspoon, drizzle the melted chocolate over the muffins and serve warm or cold.

Maple and banana cupcakes

Makes: 12
Prep: 20 minutes, plus cooling
Cook: 18–20 minutes

Banana cake invariably appeals to everyone, from tiny tots to adults. These mini ones can be served plain, simply dusted with icing sugar, or swirled with the delicious maple butter frosting.

1 small banana

2 tbsp maple syrup

2 tbsp milk

60 g/2¼ oz lightly salted butter, softened

70 g/2½ oz caster sugar

1 egg, beaten

100 g/3½ oz self-raising flour

FROSTING

150 g/5½ oz lightly salted butter, softened

1 tsp vanilla extract

6 tbsp icing sugar

7 tbsp maple syrup

8 pecan or walnut halves, roughly chopped, to decorate

1. Preheat the oven to 180°C/350°F/Gas Mark 4. Line a 12-section mini muffin tin with 3-cm/1¼-inch mini paper cases.

2. In a small mixing bowl, mash the banana to a purée with a fork. Stir in the maple syrup and milk.

3. Put the butter and caster sugar in a separate mixing bowl and beat together with an electric handheld whisk until light and fluffy. Gradually beat in the egg, a little at a time, adding a teaspoon of the flour if the mixture starts to separate.

4. Sift half the flour into the bowl containing the butter mixture, then add half the banana. Gently fold the ingredients together until only just mixed. Sift in the remaining flour, add the remaining banana mixture and fold in.

5. Spoon the mixture into the paper cases. Bake in the preheated oven for 18–20 minutes, or until risen and just firm to the touch. Leave in the tin for 5 minutes, then transfer to a wire rack to cool.

6. For the frosting, put the butter, vanilla, icing sugar and maple syrup in a bowl and beat with an electric handheld whisk until smooth and creamy. Put the frosting in a small paper piping bag fitted with a 1-cm/½-inch star nozzle and use to decorate the cupcakes. Scatter with the nuts.

Almond daisy cupcakes

Makes: 12
Prep: 25 minutes, plus cooling
Cook: 12-15 minutes

3 egg whites

40 g/1½ oz plain flour

85 g/3 oz icing sugar

70 g/2½ oz ground almonds

70 g/2½ oz lightly salted butter,
melted and cooled

DECORATION

1 quantity Lemon Buttercream
(see page 9)

red, black and lime green food
colourings

55 g/2 oz whole blanched
almonds

6 red and 6 black mini jelly beans

These fun flower cupcakes will add a welcome splash of springtime colour to the tea table. The buttercream topping is fresh and lemony, while the almond cake is moist, nutty and light.

1. Preheat the oven to 200°C/400°F/Gas Mark 6. Line a 12-section mini muffin tin with 3-cm/1¼-inch mini paper cases, preferably in red or black.

2. Whisk the eggs whites in a clean mixing bowl until they're broken up but not fluffy. Add the flour, sugar, ground almonds and butter and stir together to make a smooth paste. Spoon the mixture into the paper cases. Bake in the preheated oven for 12-15 minutes, or until risen and just firm to the touch. Leave in the tin for 5 minutes, then transfer to a wire rack.

3. For the decoration, spoon 2 tablespoons of the buttercream into a small bowl and colour with red food colouring. Spoon a further 2 tablespoons into another bowl and colour black. Colour the remaining buttercream lime green, and spread this over the cakes with a palette knife.

4. Using a sharp knife, carefully cut each blanched almond in half to make flat petal shapes. Press a jelly bean into the centre of each cake and surround with almonds, pressing them gently into the buttercream in order to shape flowers.

5. Put the red buttercream in a small paper piping bag and the black in another, and snip off the tips (see page 8). Pipe an outline around the edges of each almond, half in red and half in black.

Baby shower cupcakes

Makes: 18
Prep: 45 minutes, plus cooling
Cook: 15 minutes

70 g/2½ oz lightly salted butter,
softened

70 g/2½ oz caster sugar

1 egg

1 egg yolk

70 g/2½ oz self-raising flour

1 tsp vanilla extract

DECORATION

1 quantity Buttercream
(see page 9)

pink and blue food colourings

55 g/2 oz ready-to-roll icing

icing sugar, for dusting

These are so simple to make, but very pretty – and perfect for the next baby shower. Pink and blue look effective together, but you can change the colour scheme to any other combination.

1. Preheat the oven to 180°C/350°F/Gas Mark 4. Line 2 x 12-section mini muffin tins with 18 x 3-cm/1¼-inch mini paper cases, preferably in deep pink or blue.

2. Put the butter, caster sugar, egg, egg yolk, flour and vanilla in a mixing bowl and beat together with an electric handheld whisk until smooth and creamy. Spoon the mixture into the paper cases. Bake in the preheated oven for 15 minutes, or until risen and just firm to the touch. Leave in the tin for 5 minutes, then transfer to a wire rack to cool.

3. For the decoration, divide the buttercream equally between 2 bowls and colour 1 with pink colouring and the other with blue, so they're pale pastel. Using a palette knife, spread a thin layer of pink icing over half the cakes and blue over the other half, reserving some for decoration.

4. Colour the remaining buttercream in the bowls to a deeper tone and put it in small paper piping bags fitted with 1-cm/½-inch star nozzles. Pipe pink shells around the blue cakes and blue shells around the pink ones.

5. Colour half the ready-to-roll icing blue (see page 8) and wrap it tightly in clingfilm. Colour the remainder pink and roll it out thinly on a surface lightly dusted with icing sugar.

6. Cut the pink icing into 1-cm/½-inch wide strips, then cut across these at 2.5-cm/1-inch intervals to make tiny rectangles. Use 2 rectangles to shape bow ends, pinching the ends together as you position them on the blue-edged cakes. Bend 2 more rectangles into loops, pinching the ends together, and secure with a damp paintbrush to complete each bow. Use the blue icing in the same way to make bows for the pink-edged cakes.

Chocolate and raspberry cupcakes

Makes: 20
Prep: 50 minutes, plus cooling
Cook: 12-15 minutes

70 g/2½ oz raspberries

55 g/2 oz cocoa powder

100 ml/3½ fl oz boiling water

55 g/2 oz lightly salted butter, softened

125 g/4½ oz light muscovado sugar

1 egg, beaten

100 g/3½ oz self-raising flour

DECORATION

40 g/1½ oz lightly salted butter

100 g/3½ oz plain chocolate, roughly chopped

2 tbsp golden syrup

40 g/1½ oz raspberries

85 g/3 oz icing sugar, sifted

Here's your chance to get carried away with special messages on these pretty cakes – hearts, kisses, whatever you fancy! Once decorated they'll keep fresh for a couple of days in a cool place.

1. Preheat the oven to 180°C/350°F/Gas Mark 4. Line 2 x 12-section mini muffin tins with 20 x 3-cm/1¼-inch mini paper cases, preferably in deep pink or brown.

2. Put the raspberries in a small mixing bowl and crush with a fork until they are broken up. In a separate mixing bowl, whisk the cocoa powder with the boiling water. Leave to cool.

3. Put the butter and light muscovado sugar in a third mixing bowl and beat together with an electric handheld whisk until light and fluffy. Beat in the egg a little at a time.

4. Stir in the flour and the cocoa mixture until evenly combined, then add the raspberries and mix together lightly. Spoon the mixture into the paper cases. Bake in the preheated oven for 12-15 minutes, or until risen and just firm to the touch. Leave in the tins for 5 minutes, then transfer to a wire rack to cool.

5. For the decoration, melt the butter in a small saucepan and add the chocolate and syrup. Heat very gently until the chocolate has almost melted, then tip into a mixing bowl. Leave to cool, stirring frequently, until the mixture has thickened enough to almost hold its shape. Spoon it over the cakes and spread to the edges using a palette knife.

6. Crush the raspberries and press them through a sieve, using the back of a spoon to extract the juice. Sift the icing sugar over the juice and stir to make a loose paste. Put the icing in a small paper piping bag and snip off the tip (see page 8). Pipe hearts and kisses onto the cakes.

Red velvet heart cupcakes

Makes: 12
Prep: 1–1½ hours, plus cooling
Cook: 15 minutes

1 small raw beetroot, about
70 g/2½ oz, finely grated

1 egg

2 tbsp buttermilk or soured
cream

1 tsp vinegar

55 g/2 oz lightly salted butter,
softened

25 g/1 oz light muscovado sugar

55 g/2 oz self-raising flour

2 tsp cocoa powder

DECORATION

½ quantity Buttercream
(see page 9)

70 g/2½ oz ready-to-roll icing

deep red food colouring

icing sugar, for dusting

These cakes take a little while to decorate, but the results are gorgeous. Make yourself comfortable and enjoy!

1. Preheat the oven to 180°C/350°F/Gas Mark 4. Line a 12-section mini muffin tin with 4-cm/1½-inch mini paper cases, in deep red or white.

2. Put the beetroot, egg, buttermilk and vinegar in a mixing bowl and stir together until well combined. Put the butter and light muscovado sugar in a separate mixing bowl and beat together with an electric handheld whisk until pale and fluffy. Sift half the flour and cocoa powder into the butter mixture and tip in the beetroot mixture. Stir gently until evenly combined. Sift in the remaining flour and cocoa and stir again to mix.

3. Spoon the mixture into the paper cases. Bake in the preheated oven for 15 minutes, or until risen and just firm to the touch. Leave in the tin for 5 minutes, then transfer to a wire rack to cool.

4. For the decoration, spread the buttercream over the cakes using a palette knife. Colour the ready-to-roll icing deep red (see page 8).

5. Roll a 5 g/⅛ oz piece of icing into a thin rope 12 cm/4½ inches long. On a surface lightly dusted with icing sugar, flatten it with a rolling pin, keeping it no more than 1-cm/½-inch wide. Cut it in half lengthways, then across into 2.5-cm/1-inch pieces. Roll each little piece up between your thumb and finger to resemble a tiny rose. Use the roses to build heart shapes on top of all the cakes by pressing them gently down into the buttercream.

Petite Party Cakes

Summer flower cakes

Makes: 16
Prep: 2½ hours, plus cooling
Cook: 25 minutes

These little cakes are a labour of love, but look simply stunning. If you've planned a colour scheme for a special party, you can alter the colours of the vertical stripes to enhance your theme. Once decorated, they'll keep in a cool place for several days.

a little lightly salted butter, for greasing

1 quantity Lemon Sponge mixture (see page 9)

1 quantity Lemon Buttercream (see page 9)

900 g/2 lb white ready-to-roll icing

pink and purple food colourings

icing sugar, for dusting

1. Preheat the oven to 180°C/350°F/Gas Mark 4. Grease and base-line a cake tin containing 16 x 5-cm/2-inch sections.

2. Put a dessertspoon of the sponge mixture into each tin section. (If you have digital scales, make sure you put exactly the same amount in each section. To do this, put the prepared tin on the scales and set them to zero, then spoon 35 g/1¼ oz mixture into a section, reset the scales to zero, and fill the remaining sections, resetting the scales each time.) Bake in the preheated oven for 25 minutes, or until risen and just firm to the touch. Leave in the tin for 5 minutes before carefully loosening each cake by running a slender knife around the sides of each section. Transfer the cakes to a wire rack to cool before peeling away the base paper.

3. Reserve 3 tablespoons of the buttercream and use the remainder to spread a thin layer over the tops and sides of the cakes.

4. Reserve 300 g/10½ oz of the ready-to-roll icing. From the remainder, colour 200 g/7 oz pale pink, 200 g/7 oz purple and 200 g/7 oz a darker pink (see page 8). Take half of each coloured icing and roll it out thinly on a surface lightly dusted with icing sugar. Cut a strip from each colour that is the depth of the cakes. Cut this into 5-mm/¼-inch wide strips the depth of the cake and secure them, in alternating colours, around the sides of the cakes, pressing them gently into the buttercream. Use the remaining coloured icings to cover all the cakes.

5. Roll out the reserved white ready-to-roll icing as thinly as possible on a surface lightly dusted with icing sugar and cut out simple flower shapes using a 15-mm/½-inch plunger cutter. Press each cut flower shape out onto your finger and then place it on top of a cake. Repeat until you've built up a cluster of flowers on one cake, then repeat for all the cakes.

6. Colour the reserved buttercream pink. Put it in a small paper piping bag and snip off the tip (see page 8). Pipe little dots in the centres of all the white flowers.

White party stars

Makes: 9–10
Prep: 1–1 ½ hours, plus cooling
Cook: 25–30 minutes

unsalted butter, for greasing

1 quantity Orange Sponge
mixture (see page 9)

1 quantity Orange Buttercream
(see page 9)

400 g/14 oz white ready-to-roll
icing

1 egg white

200 g/7 oz icing sugar, sifted,
plus extra for dusting

lilac food colouring

*These pretty little stars would make a great addition
to a special occasion; you could substitute the colour
of your choice to tie in with your party theme.*

1. Preheat the oven to 180°C/350°F/Gas Mark 4. Grease and line the base
and sides of a 26-cm x 22-cm/10½-inch x 8½-inch roasting tin or similar
sized tin.

2. Turn the sponge mixture into the tin and level the surface. Bake in the
preheated oven for 25–30 minutes, or until risen and just firm to the touch.
Leave in the tin for 10 minutes, then transfer to a wire rack to cool.

3. If the cake has risen in the centre, cut off a thin slice with a large knife.
Using an 8-cm/3-inch star cutter as a guide, cut out shapes from the sponge.
(Cut each star shape as close to the previously cut star as possible so you
don't waste any sponge; freeze the sponge trimmings for making trifle or
cake pops another time.) Turn the cakes over so that the base forms a flat top.

4. Using a palette knife, spread a thin layer of buttercream over the top and
sides of each star.

5. Roll out 40 g/1½ oz ready-to-roll icing on a surface lightly dusted with
icing sugar to a circle roughly 11 cm/4½ inches in diameter. Lift it over a
star cake and fit the sides, pinching the icing together at the points. Cut off
the excess at the points and then cut around the base of the cake. Repeat
with the remaining cakes.

6. Beat the egg white in a clean bowl with the half the icing sugar until
smooth. Gradually work in the remaining icing sugar until softly peaking.
Add a little lilac food colouring and put the icing in a small paper piping
bag fitted with a little writer nozzle (see page 8). Pipe tiny dots in the centre
of the tops of the cakes.

Birthday balloons

Makes: 24
Prep: 1–1½ hours, plus cooling
Cook: 18–20 minutes

1 quantity White Chocolate
Sponge mixture (see page 9)

2 quantities Buttercream
(see page 9)

350 g/12 oz chewy sweets in
3 flavours, e.g. blackcurrant,
strawberry and orange

24 x 6-cm/2½-inch lolly sticks

100 g/3½ oz small red, green and
yellow candy-coated
chocolate sweets, such as M&Ms

Kids will love these fun, colourful cakes, lavishly decorated with tempting treats. Use candles to replace some of the balloons if you prefer.

1. Preheat the oven to 180°C/350°F/Gas Mark 4. Line 2 x 12-section mini muffin tins with 4-cm/1½-inch mini paper cases, preferably in pink, green or yellow.

2. Spoon the cake mixture into the paper cases. Bake in the preheated oven for 18–20 minutes, until risen and just firm to the touch. Leave in the tin for 5 minutes, then transfer to a wire rack to cool.

3. Using a palette knife, spread a thin layer of buttercream over the cakes.

4. For each balloon, take 8 g/⅙ oz chewy sweets (about 2 sweets) and mould them into a ball. (If they are brittle or too firm to shape, microwave them on medium power for 5–6 seconds to soften them first. Don't overheat them or they'll turn to a molten syrup.) Push each balloon shape onto the end of a lolly stick. Pinch the sweet around the stick to create the effect of a knotted end. Repeat until you have enough balloons, pushing each into a cake.

5. For the streamers, soften the remaining chewy sweets as above and roll them out thinly. Cut them into 5-cm/2-inch x 5-mm/¼-inch pieces and curl each one around a lolly stick. Twist the sweets off the sticks. Scatter the cakes with the candy-coated sweets and the sweet twists to finish.

Mini party cakes

Makes: 16
Prep: 1¼ hours, plus cooling
Cook: 40 minutes

A platter of these delicious cakes will look impressive at any special get-together. Make them a couple of days in advance, so you've got time to enjoy the decorating before more pressing party tasks arise. For a big birthday use number sparklers too.

a little lightly salted butter, for greasing

1 quantity Vanilla Sponge mixture (see page 9)

1 quantity Vanilla Buttercream (see page 9)

heart-shaped sugar sprinkles

pearl balls

1. Preheat the oven to 180°C/350°F/Gas Mark 4. Grease and line the base and sides of an 18-cm/7-inch square cake tin.

2. Spoon the cake mixture into the tin and level the surface with the back of the spoon. Bake in the preheated oven for 40 minutes, or until risen and just firm to the touch. Leave in the tin for 10 minutes, then transfer to a wire rack to cool.

3. Cut a 1-cm/½-inch crust off the edges of the cake, then cut the cake into 16 even-sized squares.

4. Put the buttercream in a paper piping bag fitted with a small star nozzle (see page 8). Place the cakes in paper cake cases.

5. Pipe vertical lines down the sides and over the top edges of the cakes. Scatter the tops of the cakes with sugar sprinkles and pearl balls.

Pupcakes

Makes: 12
Prep: 1½ hours, plus cooling
Cook: 15 minutes

70 g/2½ oz lightly salted butter,
softened, plus extra for greasing

55 g/2 oz caster sugar

70 g/2½ oz self-raising flour

1 egg

1 egg yolk

1 tsp vanilla extract

25 g/1 oz white chocolate,
finely chopped

DECORATION

300 g/10½ oz fondant icing
sugar

3 tbsp cold water

blue and black food colourings

16 white chewy sweets

8 black chewy sweets

½ quantity Buttercream
(see page 9)

small piece pink chewy sweet

small piece yellow chewy sweet

Chewy sweets are brilliant for shaping and modelling cake decorations. These cute little puppy faces will provide plenty of fun at a kids' party or special tea – the kids can even help you make them!

1. Preheat the oven to 180°C/350°F/Gas Mark 4. Place a 12-section silicone mini muffin tray on a baking tray, or grease and base-line a 12-section mini muffin tin. Put the butter, caster sugar, flour, egg, egg yolk and vanilla in a mixing bowl and beat together with an electric handheld whisk until smooth and creamy. Stir in the chocolate.

2. Using a teaspoon, spoon the mixture into the tray sections and level with the back of the spoon. Bake in the preheated oven for 15 minutes, or until risen and just firm to the touch. Leave in the tray for 5 minutes, then transfer to a wire rack to cool.

3. For the decoration, put the fondant icing sugar in a bowl and beat in 2 tablespoons of the water. Add the third tablespoon gradually, stirring with a wooden spoon until the icing is smooth and slowly drips off the back of the spoon. Stir in a little blue food colouring.

4. Dip a cake into the icing until coated. Lift the cake out of the bowl on a fork and let the excess icing drip back into the bowl before transferring the cake to the wire rack. Repeat with the remaining cakes.

5. Using a rolling pin, flatten the white chewy sweets one at a time. (If they are brittle or too firm to shape, microwave them on medium power for 5–6 seconds to soften them first. Don't overheat them or they'll turn into a molten syrup.) Using scissors, cut out rounds from the white sweets, about 4 cm/1½ inches in diameter, and secure them to the tops of the cakes using a little water.

6. Roll pea-sized balls of black chewy sweets into long, flat 'ears' (softening the sweets first as above if brittle) and position them on the cakes. Use smaller pieces for noses.

7. Beat a little black food colouring into the buttercream. Put it in a paper piping bag and snip off the tip (see page 8). Use to pipe eyes, a mouth and whiskers onto each face. Use the pink chewy sweets to shape tongues and yellow chewy sweets to shape collars. If liked, shape small bones from the leftover white chews and rest them next to the cakes.

Halloween cakes

Makes: 18
Prep: 1½ hours, plus cooling
Cook: 40 minutes

a little lightly salted butter, for
greasing

2 quantities Orange Sponge
mixture (see page 9)

2 tbsp lemon juice

2 tbsp orange juice

3 tbsp runny honey

6 tbsp apricot jam

2 tbsp hot water

orange food colouring

750 g/1 lb 10 oz white ready-to-
roll icing

icing sugar, for dusting

55 g/2 oz plain chocolate, roughly
chopped

several soft green jellies

20 small Oreo cookies, filling
removed

Serve these cakes at a Halloween party, or box them up for impressive 'take home' gifts. They look particularly stunning on a dark plate or cloth.

1. Preheat the oven to 180°C/350°F/Gas Mark 4. Grease and line the base and sides of a 26-cm x 22-cm/10½-inch x 8½-inch roasting tin or similar sized tin. Grease the baking paper.

2. Turn the cake mixture into the tin and level the surface. Bake in the preheated oven for 40 minutes, or until risen and just firm to the touch. Leave in the tin for 10 minutes, then transfer to a wire rack to cool.

3. If the cake has risen in the centre, cut off a thin slice with a large knife. Using a 6-cm/2½-inch half-moon cutter as a guide, cut out shapes from the sponge. Turn the cakes over so that the base forms a flat top.

4. Mix the juices with the honey in a small jug and drizzle over the surface of the cakes so the syrup seeps into the sponge. Press the jam through a small sieve into a bowl and stir in the hot water. Brush this mixture over the tops and sides of the cakes.

5. Knead orange food colouring into the ready-to-roll icing (see page 8). Roll out 40 g/1½ oz of the icing on a surface lightly dusted with icing sugar to an oval 15 cm x 10 cm/6 inches x 4 inches. Lift it over a half-moon cake and fit it around the sides, pinching the icing together at the points. Cut off the excess at these points and then cut around the base of the cake. Repeat with the remaining cakes, reserving the icing trimmings.

6. Put the chocolate in a heatproof bowl, set the bowl over a saucepan of gently simmering water and heat until melted. Put the chocolate in a small paper piping bag and snip off the tip (see page 8). Colour the icing trimmings a deeper orange and shape them into small balls. Mark 'pumpkin' ridges with the back of a knife. Cut small pieces of soft jelly and push them into the tops for stalks, securing with chocolate.

7. To shape bats, heat an Oreo cookie in the microwave until it's soft (this will take 1½–2 minutes, but check after a minute). Cut a circle from one side with a 2.5-cm/1-inch cutter. Cut small flutes from the opposite sides with a 1.5-cm/½-inch cutter. Secure the decorations in place with chocolate and pipe bat eyes and extra bats around the sides of the cakes.

Party presents

Makes: 16
Prep: 1½ hours, plus cooling
and decorating
Cook: 45 minutes

a little lightly salted butter, for greasing

1 quantity White Chocolate or Almond Sponge mixture
(see page 9)

1 quantity Buttercream
(see page 9)

8 tbsp apricot jam

2 tbsp brandy, almond or orange liqueur or water

850 g/1 lb 14 oz white marzipan

green, blue and pink food colourings

icing sugar, for dusting

55 g/2 oz white chocolate, roughly chopped

3 metres/10 feet deep pink ribbon, about 1-cm/½-inch wide

3 metres/10 feet yellow ribbon, about 5-mm/¼-inch wide

Marzipan makes a great cake covering, particularly for those who find the sweetness of icing too much. It can be coloured, rolled, cut out and shaped just as you would ready-to-roll icing, and is equally fun to work with.

1. Preheat the oven to 180°C/350°F/Gas Mark 4. Grease and line the base and sides of an 18-cm/7-inch square cake tin. Turn the cake mixture out into the tin and level the surface. Bake in the preheated oven for 45 minutes, or until risen and just firm to the touch. Leave in the tin for 10 minutes, then transfer to a wire rack to cool.

2. If the cake has risen in the centre, cut off a thin slice with a large knife so that the surface of the cake is level. Split the cake in half horizontally and sandwich the halves together with the buttercream. Cut a 5-mm/¼-inch crust off the sides. Turn the cake over and check that it's completely level. Cut the cake into 16 even-sized squares.

3. Press the jam through a small sieve into a little saucepan and stir in the brandy. Heat gently until smooth. Colour 25 g/1 oz of the marzipan green (see page 8) and another 25 g/1 oz blue and reserve both, wrapped separately in clingfilm. Colour the remaining marzipan pale pink. Brush the apricot glaze all over the tops and sides of the cake squares.

4. Roll out 55 g/2 oz of the pink marzipan thinly on a surface lightly dusted with icing sugar, to a 12-cm/4½-inch square. Lift it over a cake and fit it down the sides, pinching the excess together at the corners. Cut off the excess at these corners and then cut around the base of the cake. Repeat with the remaining cakes, reserving the marzipan trimmings.

5. Colour the marzipan trimmings a deeper shade of pink and use, with the other coloured marzipans, to shape parcels. Arrange on the cakes.

6. Put the chocolate in a heatproof bowl, set the bowl over a saucepan of gently simmering water and heat until melted. Put the melted chocolate in a small paper piping bag and snip off the tip (see page 8). Pipe lines over the parcels and around the top edges of the cakes. Cut the pink ribbon into 19-cm/7½-inch lengths and secure around the bases of the cakes with dots of chocolate from the piping bag. Cut the yellow ribbon into the same sized lengths and position these so they sit in the centre of the pink ribbon, again secured with dots of the chocolate.

Mini ivory wedding cakes

Makes: 16
Prep: 1½ hours, plus cooling
Cook: 1 hour

Make these pretty cakes for a girls' night before the big day, or of course for the wedding party itself. Bake the sponges a day before decorating so they've time to firm up a bit. Assemble the cakes a day before the party.

a little lightly salted butter, for greasing

2 quantities White Chocolate Sponge mixture (see page 9)

250 g/9 oz white ready-to-roll icing

brown or ivory food colouring

icing sugar, for dusting

16 x 7.5-cm/3-inch round silver cake cards

300 ml/10 fl oz double cream

300 g/10½ oz white chocolate, roughly chopped

10 metres (33 feet) wired organza ribbon, about
2.5 cm/1 inch wide

1. Preheat the oven to 180°C/350°F/Gas Mark 4. Grease and line the base and sides of a 23-cm/9-inch square cake tin.

2. Spoon two-thirds of the cake mixture into the tin and level the surface with the back of the spoon. Bake in the preheated oven for 35 minutes, or until well risen and just firm to the touch. Leave in the tin for 10 minutes, then transfer to a wire rack to cool. Wash and reline the tin and bake the remaining mixture for 20–25 minutes, as before.

3. Colour the ready-to-roll icing with a dash of brown food colouring (see page 8). Roll out half the icing as thinly as possible on a surface lightly dusted with icing sugar. Cut out 8 rounds using a 7.5-cm/3-inch cookie cutter, re-rolling the trimmings to make sufficient. Repeat with the other half. Dampen the surfaces of the cake cards and position a circle of icing on each.

4. To make a ganache, heat half the cream in a small saucepan until very hot but not boiling. Pour it into a mixing bowl and add the chocolate. Leave to stand, stirring frequently, until the chocolate has melted. Leave to cool completely. Stir in the remaining cream and beat lightly with an electric handheld whisk on a slow speed until the ganache is just thick enough to hold its shape. (If over-whisked it might start to separate.)

5. Using a 5-cm/2-inch round cookie cutter as a guide, cut out 16 rounds from the deeper sponge cake. Use a 3-cm/1½-inch round cutter as a guide to cut out 16 rounds from the shallower sponge. (Freeze the trimmings for making trifle or cake pops another time.) Place the larger cakes on the iced cards, securing with a little ganache. Spread some of the remaining ganache over the tops and sides of these cakes with a palette knife. Position the smaller cakes on top and cover these with ganache in the same way. Leave to set in a cool place for 1–2 hours.

6. Cut the ribbon into 60-cm/24-inch lengths and wrap a length around each cake, securing at the tops with bows and cutting off any long ends.

Little Fabulous Cakes

Mini cake pops

Makes: 24
Prep: 1–1¼ hours, plus setting
Cook: 40 minutes

These mini 'cupcake' cake pops have both child and adult appeal, so they're ideal for a gathering of mixed ages. Once iced, they'll keep in a cool place for a couple of days.

450 g/1 lb cooked Vanilla or Almond Sponge (see page 9) or shop-bought

85 g/3 oz mascarpone cheese

70 g/2½ oz icing sugar

½ tsp vanilla or almond extract

DECORATION

225 g/8 oz milk chocolate, roughly chopped

24 lolly sticks

150 g/5½ oz fondant icing sugar

pink food colouring

4 tsp cold water

24 small sweets, such as mini M&Ms

sugar sprinkles

1. Line a baking tray with baking paper. Crumble the sponge cake into a mixing bowl. Add the mascarpone, icing sugar and vanilla and mix together until you have a thick paste.

2. Roll a 25 g/1 oz piece of the paste into a ball. Push this ball into a mini paper case, pressing it down so that when it is removed from the case you have a mini cupcake shape. Shape the remaining 23 cake pops in the same way. Place on the baking tray and chill for 1–2 hours to firm up.

3. Put the chocolate in a heatproof bowl, set the bowl over a saucepan of gently simmering water and heat until melted. Remove from the heat. Push a lolly stick into each cake pop. Dip a cake pop into the chocolate, turning it until coated. Lift it from the bowl, letting the excess drip back into the bowl, then place it in a cup or tumbler. Repeat with the remaining cake pops. Chill or leave in a cool place until the chocolate has set.

4. Put the fondant icing sugar in a mixing bowl and beat in a dash of pink food colouring and the water until smooth. The icing should almost hold its shape. Spoon a little onto a cake pop, easing it slightly down the sides with the side of a teaspoon. If the icing is too firm you might need to add a dash more water. Before the icing sets, place a small sweet in the centre of each cake pop and scatter with sugar sprinkles.

Snowman cake pops

Makes: 20

Prep: 1¼ –1½ hours, plus setting

200 g/7 oz shop-bought angel
cake

300 g/10½ oz icing sugar

4 tbsp double cream

2 tsp peppermint extract

DECORATION

300 g/10½ oz fondant icing
sugar, plus extra for piping

20 lolly sticks

3 tbsp cold water

black, orange, red and yellow
food colourings

100 g/3½ oz marzipan

Whether it's a winter birthday, Christmas or New Year, these fun seasonal cake pops are perfect – especially if there's snow on the ground!

1. Line a baking tray with baking paper. Crumble the angel cake into a mixing bowl. Add the icing sugar, cream and peppermint extract and mix together until you have a thick paste, adding a dash more cream if the mixture feels too dry.

2. Roll a 20 g/¾ oz piece of the paste into a ball and shape the remaining 19 snowman bases in the same way. Now roll 20 x 5 g/⅛ oz pieces of the paste into balls. Press a small ball onto a larger one to shape a snowman, and repeat for the remaining snowmen. Place on the baking tray and chill for 1-2 hours to firm up.

3. Put the fondant icing sugar in a mixing bowl and beat in the water to make a paste that coats the back of a spoon in a thin layer. Push a lolly stick through each snowman so it goes halfway into the smaller ball (various types of lolly sticks are available; use traditional white or wooden ones; sturdy bamboo skewers can also be used or a pack of chop sticks).

4. Dip a snowman in the icing, turning it until coated. Lift it from the bowl, letting the excess drip back into the bowl, then place it in a cup or tumbler. Repeat with the remaining snowmen, reserving some icing.

5. Beat a dash of black food colouring and a little extra icing sugar into the icing left in the bowl so the mixture is thick enough to hold its shape. Put the icing in a small paper piping bag and snip off the tip (see page 8).

6. Colour a cherry-sized ball of marzipan orange (see page 8), then half the remainder red and half yellow. Use the red and yellow marzipan to shape tiny hats and scarves, pressing them into the fondant icing to secure. Shape and secure pointed noses in orange marzipan. Pipe eyes, mouths and buttons using the black icing.

Chocolate mint cake pops

Makes: 26–28
Prep: 1 hour, plus setting
Cook: 5 minutes

This is a cake pop version of 'rocky road', and is about as easy to make as it gets! The milk chocolate coating has family appeal, but you can use plain chocolate instead for a more adult flavour.

300 g/10½ oz plain chocolate, roughly chopped

25 g/1 oz unsalted butter, softened

50 g/1¾ oz hard-boiled mint sweets

450 g/1 lb milk chocolate

50 g/1¾ oz mini marshmallows, roughly chopped

26–28 lolly sticks

chocolate sprinkles, to decorate

1. Line a baking tray with baking paper. Put the plain chocolate in a heatproof bowl, set the bowl over a saucepan of gently simmering water and heat until melted. Stir in the butter. Leave until the mixture is cool but not beginning to set.

2. Put the mint sweets in a polythene bag and tap firmly with a rolling pin until they are broken into tiny pieces. Finely chop 150 g/5½ oz of the milk chocolate, then stir it into the melted plain chocolate with the mints and marshmallows until thoroughly mixed.

3. As soon as the mixture is firm enough to hold its shape, roll 20 g/¾ oz of it into a ball. Shape the remaining cake pops in the same way. Place them on the baking tray and chill for 30–60 minutes, until firm but not brittle. Push a lolly stick into each cake pop, then chill for 10 minutes.

4. Roughly chop the remaining milk chocolate and melt as above, then remove from the heat. Dip a cake pop into the chocolate, turning it until coated. Lift it from the bowl, letting the excess drip back into the bowl, and place it in a cup or tumbler. Sprinkle with chocolate sprinkles. Repeat with the remaining cake pops. Chill or leave in a cool place until the chocolate has set.

2

3

4

Chocolate 'ice-cream' cones

Makes: 16

Prep: 40 minutes, plus setting

125 g/4½ oz milk chocolate, roughly chopped

200 ml/7 fl oz double cream

2 tbsp vanilla sugar

chocolate and rainbow sugar sprinkles, to decorate

MOUSSE

200 g/7 oz plain chocolate, roughly chopped

4 tbsp water

2 egg whites

25 g/1 oz caster sugar

These mini chocolate cones are filled with a delicious chocolate mousse and topped with swirls of whipped cream. Unlike regular ice-creams, they won't melt if left out of the freezer!

1. Line a baking tray with baking paper. To shape the cones, cut 8 circles of baking paper using a 17-cm/7-inch plate or cake tin as a guide. Fold the circles in half and then cut them in half just to one side of the fold. Shape each semi-circle into a cone so the straight edges meet to create a cone of double thickness paper, securing it in place with sticky tape.

2. Put the milk chocolate in a heatproof bowl, set the bowl over a pan of gently simmering water and heat until melted. Place a teaspoon of melted chocolate into a cone so that it's about a third full and spread the chocolate up the sides using a pastry brush. Invert it onto the baking tray and chill for at least 30 minutes, until set.

3. To make the mousse, put the plain chocolate and water in a heatproof bowl, set the bowl over a pan of gently simmering water and heat until melted. Whisk the egg whites in a clean mixing bowl until peaking. Whisk in the caster sugar, a little at a time. Tip the melted chocolate onto the whites and fold together with a spatula. Spoon the mousse into the cones and chill for 1 hour.

4. Whip the cream with the vanilla sugar until only just peaking. Put it into a small piping bag fitted with a 1-cm/½-inch star nozzle. Peel the paper from the cones and pipe swirls of cream on top. Scatter with sprinkles.

Double chocolate whoopie pies

Makes: 12–14
Prep: 25 minutes, plus cooling
Cook: 10 minutes

70 g/2½ oz lightly salted
butter, softened

125 g/4½ oz light muscovado
sugar

1 egg

1 tsp vanilla extract

125 g/4½ oz plain flour

½ tsp bicarbonate of soda

40 g/1½ oz cocoa powder

150 ml/5 fl oz buttermilk

FILLING

200 g/7 oz milk chocolate,
roughly chopped

140 g/5 oz unsalted butter,
softened

85 g/3 oz icing sugar

70 g/2½ oz plain chocolate,
roughly chopped

chocolate sprinkles, optional

Quench your chocolate craving with these moist and morish homemade whoopies; they're so good they'll be gone before you know it!

1. Preheat the oven to 200°C/400°F/Gas Mark 6. Line 2 baking trays with baking paper. Put the lightly salted butter, light muscovado sugar, egg and vanilla in a mixing bowl and beat together with an electric handheld whisk until the mixture is thickened and pale.

2. Sift the flour, bicarbonate of soda and cocoa into a separate mixing bowl. Add half of this mixture and half the buttermilk to the butter mixture. Stir with a spatula or large metal spoon. Once combined, add the remaining flour mixture and buttermilk and carefully stir again.

3. Put the mixture into a large piping bag fitted with a 1-cm/½-inch plain nozzle (see page 8). Pipe small blobs onto the baking trays, slicing off the peaks with a small knife and spacing the blobs about 5 cm/2 inches apart to allow for expansion.

4. Bake in the preheated oven for 10 minutes, or until risen and just firm to the touch, switching over the baking trays halfway through cooking. Leave on the trays for 5 minutes, then transfer to a wire rack to cool.

5. For the filling, put the milk chocolate in a heatproof bowl, set the bowl over a saucepan of gently simmering water and heat until melted. Leave to cool slightly. Put the unsalted butter and icing sugar in a mixing bowl and beat with an electric handheld whisk until light and fluffy. Stir the melted chocolate into the butter mixture until evenly combined.

6. Sandwich the whoopie pies together in pairs with the filling. Melt the plain chocolate as above, then drizzle a little of it over each whoopie pie. Scatter with the sprinkles, if using. Leave in a cool place to firm up for a couple of hours.

Gingerbread and vanilla whoopie pies

Makes: 14
Prep: 25 minutes, plus cooling
Cook: 10 minutes

These whoopies have a distinctive gingerbread flavour, perfect for autumnal comfort eating!

1 egg

70 g/2½ oz light muscovado sugar

1 tbsp black treacle

40 g/1½ oz lightly salted butter, melted

5 tbsp milk

150 g/5 oz plain flour

½ tsp bicarbonate of soda

1½ tsp ground ginger

½ tsp ground mixed spice

FILLING

100 g/3½ oz cream cheese

15 g/½ oz unsalted butter, softened

1 tsp vanilla extract

55 g/2 oz icing sugar, plus extra for dusting

1 tsp boiling water

1. Preheat the oven to 180°C/350°F/Gas Mark 4. Line 2 baking trays with baking paper. Put the egg, light muscovado sugar and treacle in a mixing bowl and beat together with an electric handheld whisk until thickened and foamy. Beat in the lightly salted butter and milk.

2. Sift the flour, bicarbonate of soda, ginger and mixed spice into the bowl and stir with a wooden spoon to make a soft paste.

3. Spoon teaspoons of the mixture onto the baking trays, flattening them slightly so each spoonful is about 3 cm/1¼ inches in diameter. Space the spoonfuls about 5 cm/2 inches apart to allow for expansion.

4. Bake in the preheated oven for 10 minutes, or until risen and firm to the touch, switching over the baking trays halfway through cooking. Leave on the trays for 5 minutes, then transfer to a wire rack to cool.

5. For the filling, put the cream cheese, unsalted butter, vanilla and icing sugar in a mixing bowl and beat together with an electric handheld whisk until smooth and creamy. Beat in the boiling water to soften. Sandwich the whoopie pies together in pairs with the filling. Leave in a cool place to firm up for a couple of hours, then dust with icing sugar.

Index